The Battle of Lexington and Concord

BY NEIL JOHNSON

FOUR WINDS PRESS ❊ NEW YORK
Maxwell Macmillan Canada   Toronto
Maxwell Macmillan International
New York   Oxford   Singapore   Sydney

ACKNOWLEDGMENTS   Special thanks to Mark Nichipor of the Minute Man National Historic Park for checking the facts in this book. The author would also like to thank the following for helping make the images in this book possible:

The rangers and staff of the Minute Man
   National Historic Park
Massachusetts Council of Minute Men
Lexington Minute Men
Concord Minute Men
His Majesty's 10th Regiment of Foot
His Majesty's 22nd Regiment of Foot

His Majesty's 42nd Regiment of Foot
His Majesty's 1st Regiment of Footguards
Boston Tea Party Ship and Museum
Boston's Old North Church
Lawrence and William Kenney
David Hardt

The photographs illustrating this book were made during April of both 1990 and 1991 at the annual reenactments of the fighting at Lexington Green and Concord's North Bridge, and during the Battle Road reenactment of 1991. Readers should know that the reenactments are staged on the historic sites. Though the North Bridge is a reconstruction, the Old North Church and Jason Russell House are the actual historic structures.

To Janet Butcher and Manelle Weaver,
history teachers, who deserve to be mentioned
in at least one history book

Introduction

THE AMERICAN REVOLUTION began in Lexington and Concord, two Massachusetts towns, on Wednesday, April 19, 1775. On that day, no one knew that a war, which would take years to finish, had begun. No one fighting knew that what had started would end in the birth of a new country. This would be a war like no other: one fought for political reasons. Wars until then had been fought for other reasons—for land, for money, for power. But this war would be fought for an idea: the belief that a people should be free to govern themselves.

Over centuries, trees grow to old age and die, wooden bridges can no longer support loads and are replaced, rivers slowly change course, and buildings crumble or are torn down to make room for new ones. The progress of civilization and nature can cover up the places where history has been made. But when the events are important enough and when people care enough, these places can be preserved for each new generation.

Today anyone is able to walk on the ground where those historic events of April 19, 1775, took place. Each year, on the anniversary of that day, thousands of people witness reenactments of the fighting. People who call themselves "living historians," some descended from the original participants in the battle, dress as the rebels and British of 1775 and arm themselves with reproductions of eighteenth-century muskets to reenact the beginning of the American Revolution.

But this time, though the black powder explodes violently in the muskets, no musket balls hiss through the air. No blood stains the ground.

By modern standards, the number of men killed and wounded on both sides in the day's fighting was very low. The British had 73 killed, 174 wounded, and 26 missing. The Americans had 49 killed, 40 wounded, and 5 missing.

There were two reasons for these low casualty figures. The muskets that were used, which shot large lead balls, were very inaccurate; and both sides, for the most part, did their shooting at some distance from each other, with the patriots behind protective cover.

Yet the unthinkable had happened on that April day: American colonists had taken up arms against the forces of their king. From this conflict would arise a civil war: the war for independence. As a historian writing of Concord years later would comment, "A traveler on this spot . . . cannot fail of being deeply affected by a comparison of so small a beginning with so mighty an issue."

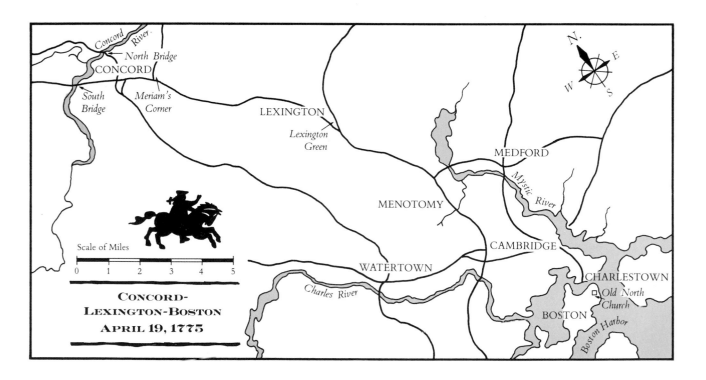

CONCORD-
LEXINGTON-BOSTON
APRIL 19, 1775

THE AMERICANS AT LEXINGTON did not want to fight. They gripped their muskets tightly but did not raise them, as they stood nervously watching while more and more soldiers in bright red uniforms hurried off the road and lined up on the village green to face them.

The rebels had been warned that the British soldiers were coming. The rebels had been up most of the night waiting and they were confused. What were *they*—a small company of armed farmers—doing standing up against an army from England, one of the most powerful countries in the world?

AT THE BEGINNING OF THE 1700s, the people living in the thirteen British colonies along the Atlantic coast of North America were loyal citizens of the Crown of England. They were starting to enjoy the colonial life. The populations of the cities along the coast were expanding quickly; their seaports bustled with activity, and farms everywhere thrived. The Native Americans could not stop the rapid colonization, and those who refused to be subjugated were pushed farther and farther westward. King George and the British Parliament ruled with a long arm from across the Atlantic.

But the rich and open land and the good life began to change the colonists. Those who were eligible to vote elected their own local governments, making their own decisions on how to live their lives and conduct their businesses. British government officials did not understand these changes. They gave Americans no representation in Parliament. And they ordered them to pay more and more taxes to cover the huge costs of the French and Indian War, which ended in 1763.

England had won Canada from France, and Florida from Spain, in that war. England had also left 10,000 royal troops in the American colonies, after the war was over. Many colonists wondered what these soldiers were protecting them against.

By the early 1770s, most colonists saw England as a stern and unfair parent whose laws, taxes, and troops were threatening their freedom. The king and Parliament saw the colonists as rowdy children with no respect for rules. It did not help to have 3,000 miles of ocean between them.

As time went on, each side became angrier and angrier with the other. The more the colonists protested the various taxes, the harsher the British reaction became. Many colonists began to actively resist British rule in any way they could.

The city with the most anti-British activity was the busy seaport of Boston in the colony of Massachusetts. There, patriot leaders such as the lawyer John Adams and his outspoken cousin, the fiery politician Samuel Adams, the rich John Hancock, and the popular Dr. Joseph Warren spoke out against the British government at every chance. They were enraged when, in 1773, England passed a law changing the way tea was sold to the colonies. This so-called Tea Act said that only one company—the East India Company, which was British—could sell tea in America. American merchants could no longer take part in this profitable business.

In some port cities, Americans refused to unload the ships carrying the East India Company's tea. Boston patriots went further. On the night before the tea was to be unloaded, patriots—many disguised as Indians—boarded the three tea ships in Boston harbor and threw the hated cargo into the water. The night's actions became known as the Boston Tea Party.

Finally, in 1774, the situation in Boston became so bad that Parliament punished the people of the city by passing an act that completely shut down its port. Thousands of soldiers were sent in to keep order. Several other acts intended to punish the rebellious colonies and limit their freedom followed. Parliament also

named General Thomas Gage, the commander in chief of the British troops in the colonies, as governor of Massachusetts.

The other colonies rallied to the support of Massachusetts. At the First Continental Congress, in September of 1774, delegates from every colony except Georgia met in Philadelphia. There, as well as taking other actions, they encouraged the colonies to prepare for war.

For over a hundred years, all colonial towns had maintained local militias—temporary citizen soldiers—to protect their immediate areas. In Massachusetts, these militias became more active, in preparation for a possible fight. In 1774, a quarter of each militia was trained to be armed and ready to fight at a minute's notice. These soldiers were called minutemen.

With nothing to do in the closed-down city of Boston, the patriots had plenty of people with enough time on their hands to watch British military activities closely. Spies were placed everywhere to listen in on British soldiers and report anything unusual back to the patriot leaders.

For safety's sake, John Hancock and Samuel Adams had decided to conduct their rebel work from outside of Boston. Paul Revere, a skilled silversmith and respected patriot leader himself, became a regular messenger, riding from Boston into the countryside to report British activities to Hancock and Adams, his good friends.

Early in 1775, the British learned of large numbers of cannons, barrels of gunpowder, and other military supplies being collected and stored by the rebels in various rural locations. On April 14, General Gage received a letter from England, ordering him to take action against this rebellious activity. About twenty miles from Boston, the small town of Concord was known to be one of the storage places.

General Gage ordered Lieutenant Colonel Francis Smith to prepare to lead about 700 British troops to Concord. Though the plans were to be top secret, patriot spies soon learned of them. Revere arranged a signal to let watching patriots know when and how Smith's men would be traveling. If they set out over land, a single lantern would be hung in the steeple of Boston's North Church. Two lanterns would mean the troops were shortening their trip by crossing the harbor in boats.

During the evening of April 18, Smith's troops began gathering in Boston, preparing to leave the city—in boats. Revere asked a friend to hang two lanterns in the church steeple, then quietly rowed a small boat across the harbor. He borrowed a horse and set off at a gallop to warn the town of Concord—as well as Hancock and Adams, who were staying in the nearby town of Lexington—that the British were coming.

Revere was not the only messenger riding that night. William Dawes, a young shoemaker, had already ridden off on the same urgent mission over a different route. Dr. Warren had sent both riders out, just in case one was captured.

At the farmhouses and homes of militia leaders along the way to Lexington, Revere and Dawes cried out their warning. The minutemen dressed quickly, grabbed their muskets, and bid their families good-bye. They headed immediately to their prearranged meeting places, some riding off themselves to warn others.

At about midnight, Revere—followed soon after by Dawes—arrived to wake the Lexington household where Hancock and Adams were staying. Then Revere and Dawes set off toward Concord. On the road, the two were joined by Dr. Samuel Prescott, a Concord patriot who had been in Lexington courting a lady friend.

Between Lexington and Concord, a group of British officers ambushed the three riders and captured Revere. Dawes escaped, but he had to turn back toward Lexington. Prescott also escaped in the early-morning darkness and managed to continue on to warn the Concord militia.

AFTER RECEIVING REVERE'S WARNING, the Lexington militia, commanded by Captain John Parker, gathered quickly on the town green. Parker's men nervously paced the grass in the darkness for over an hour before Parker allowed those who lived nearby to go back home. Others went to Buckman's Tavern, next to the green. All were instructed to return if they heard the militia drums.

It had taken the British army so long to cross the harbor and get started on their march that Colonel Smith knew the countryside had probably been warned of his "secret" march. He sent back word to General Gage in Boston, asking for more troops to be sent as reinforcements. Throughout the day, Smith's men would wait desperately for those reinforcements while the American forces grew steadily.

Every hour or so, Captain Parker sent a rider down the road for news on the British position. Each time, however, the British captured the rider. Finally, as dawn began to push back the darkness, word came back to Parker that the troops were approaching Lexington from just down the road. Drums rolled. The militia re-formed quickly on the green. A small crowd of unarmed onlookers gathered nearby.

Major John Pitcairn led the advance guard of the British army into Lexington, with Smith and the main body of troops not far behind. After marching for miles in the middle of the night, Pitcairn's men were tired and testy. They had been sitting in Boston for many months with nothing to do but develop a hatred for the "impudent" rebels.

Pitcairn had intended only to march through Lexington and continue on to Concord, but he decided first to disarm and disperse the militia lined up on the green. He ordered his men into an attack formation. Eager for action, the redcoats rushed onto the green, shouting excitedly.

The Americans watched in silence.

"Disperse, ye rebels! Lay down your arms and disperse!" called out Major Pitcairn from his horse.

Captain Parker did not like what he saw. His militia of about seventy men was in great danger before the larger force of redcoats. There was only one thing to do. He gave the order to disperse. A few stubborn men stood their ground, facing the British, but most of the men turned and began walking away, although they did not lay down their muskets.

At that moment, everyone heard the sound of a gunshot over the noise of the redcoats. No one would ever be sure who fired the shot.

Both the militia and the redcoats had been given strict orders not to fire first, but someone *had* fired. Without waiting for orders, the redcoats immediately fired two deadly volleys into the dispersing militia. Major Pitcairn angrily signaled them with his sword to cease firing, but his soldiers took no notice.

In the confusion that followed, a few of the militia managed to shoot back at the redcoats, but with little effect. The redcoats then charged the rebels, and the militia, as well as the onlookers, fled in fear and shock.

In a few short minutes, eight Americans died and ten were wounded. Militia bullets struck one redcoat and Major Pitcairn's horse, but these wounds were not serious. A redcoat bayonet killed the already wounded Jonas Parker, an elderly cousin of the captain, while he tried to reload his gun in the middle of the green. Jonathan Harrington, mortally wounded, managed to crawl back to his nearby home, where he died on the doorstep before his wife's eyes.

With the enemy driven off, Major Pitcairn finally managed to gather his troops together, and they resumed the march on Concord with the rest of the British army. But with the dead and dying militia members lying in the wet grass, Pitcairn first allowed the soldiers a rousing cheer, a British tradition after a victory.

IN THE MEANTIME, word of the approaching redcoats spread quickly throughout the area. Many other town militias had gathered and were already marching for Concord, unaware that blood had been spilled on the green at Lexington.

Concord, five miles away, had been aroused by Prescott's alarm. The town militia had formed, summoned by the ringing of a church bell. Everyone worked hard to bury or otherwise hide the tons of gunpowder, lead musket balls, cannons, and food. Workers had loaded up every available cart with supplies. Minutemen from neighboring towns began arriving to join in the work. A messenger

who had been sent to Lexington returned to say that he had seen redcoats and heard gunfire in the town.

The militia set off down the road to Lexington to observe the enemy. When the Americans saw the long, red-coated columns advancing, bayonets flashing in the sun, the colonists turned and marched back toward Concord, with the British not far behind.

Both groups of marchers used fifes and drums to stay in step and to keep up their spirits. The road into Concord became a parade of marching men, complete with rumbling drums and lively music.

Many of the rebels wanted to make a stand in the center of town. A fiery Concord minister, the Reverend William Emerson, is said to have declared, "Let us stand our ground. If we die, let us die here!" But Colonel James Barrett, the commander of the Concord militia, saw that the 700 or so British troops far outnumbered his 150 men. He positioned his men on a small ridge that looked down on the road and the town.

When Colonel Smith sent some of his British troops toward the town along this ridge, the militia moved to a second ridge, which ran along the road leading to the wooden North Bridge. Smith's men occupied this ridge as well, and the militia—still avoiding any conflict—moved up the road and over the bridge, which crossed the Concord River. They took up a new position on Punkatassett Hill, overlooking the bridge.

Half of the company of redcoats that had been following the militia took possession of the North Bridge. The other half of this group went on up the road past the militia, to search Colonel Barrett's farm for military supplies. But Barrett had galloped swiftly home ahead of the troops to help hide the cases of ammunition stored there. The redcoats would find very little at his farm.

Other British troops went to guard the town's South Bridge. The rest of the redcoats remained in the center of town, destroying any military supplies they could find. While they were thorough in their search, they hesitated to destroy any private property. The soldiers passed over a large quantity of flour after a townsman pretended that it belonged to his mill and not to the militia. Some supplies were found; most of them were not.

As the morning wore on, more and more militiamen from the surrounding towns arrived to join those gathered on Punkatassett Hill. The number of American soldiers grew to about 400.

THE BRITISH SOLDIERS guarding the North Bridge were led by Captain Walter Sloane Laurie. As he eyed the increasing number of rebels, Captain Laurie sent word to Colonel Smith for more troops. They would arrive far too late.

In Concord, several of the hidden cannons were found and taken out onto the town square, where the iron barrels were damaged, making them useless. The British soldiers then broke up the wooden cannon carriages, placed them in a pile, and put a torch to the wood. A plume of thick, black smoke rose from the fire into the sky.

To the Concord men who had been waiting uneasily on the hill for an hour, the smoke became very troubling. At about half past nine, one man went to the just-returned Colonel Barrett and asked, "Will you let them burn the town down?" Barrett and the other militia leaders agreed that action was necessary. They would take the North Bridge from the redcoats and march into town.

With Barrett reminding them several times not to fire unless the redcoats fired first, the men solemnly set off down the hill toward the bridge.

Three men led the column: Captain Isaac Davis of Acton, Major John Buttrick of Concord, and Lieutenant Colonel John Robinson of Westford. Because his own men had not yet arrived, the higher-ranking Robinson gave Buttrick command of the attack.

As there had never before been a real battle between American militia and British redcoats, neither side knew what to expect. High, sweet fife music was the only accompaniment to the sound of marching feet.

As soon as the militia began gathering to advance toward the bridge, the British force of about eighty men positioned themselves on the militia's side of the bridge. They soon realized that this was an unwise position, as this time the

Americans far outnumbered the redcoats. They quickly crossed to the Concord side and turned to defend themselves.

As the Americans approached, a few redcoats began taking up some of the wooden planks of the bridge, but they realized there was not time to take out enough planks to stop the militia's advance. The Americans were almost at the bridge.

The British first fired several warning shots into the Concord River. Finally the redcoats let loose a thunderous volley. Captain Davis and another militiaman from Acton fell dead upon the road.

"Fire, fellow soldiers, for God's sake, fire!" cried Buttrick to the men behind him.

The militiamen raised their muskets and fired into the redcoat ranks. Smoke filled the air as hundreds of lead musket balls flew over the Concord River. After a very brief exchange of fire, the outnumbered British turned and retreated headlong back into the town to join the rest of the army. They left behind one soldier dead on the road and one seriously wounded. They carried several other wounded soldiers back to Concord, one of whom soon died.

The retreating redcoats were met by their tardy reinforcements, led by Colonel Smith. "Being a very fat, heavy man," a British officer later complained about the slow-moving colonel, "he would not have reached the bridge in half an hour, though it was not half a mile to it."

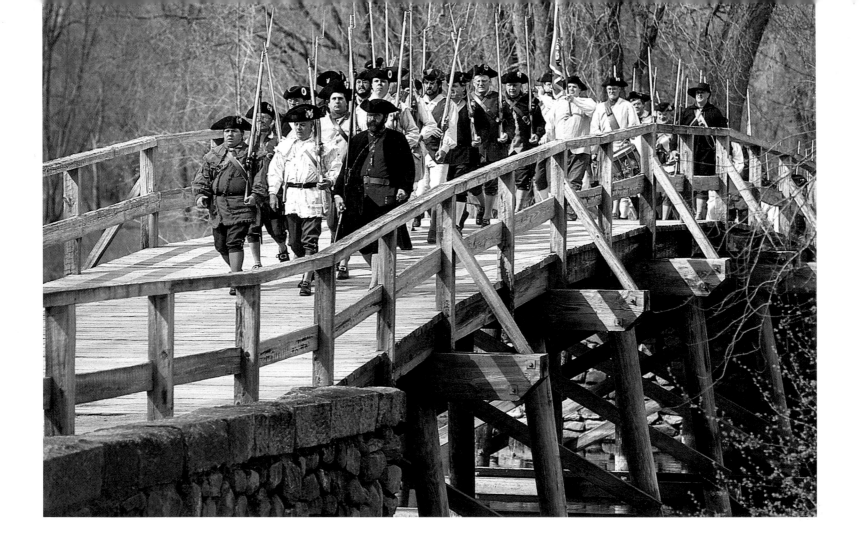

The Americans continued to march forward over the bridge, then stopped to gather on the ridge nearby to decide what to do next. In the lull, a young patriot, armed only with a hatchet, crossed the bridge to join the main body of men on the ridge. Upon finding the wounded redcoat, he struck him a death blow to the head and continued on.

The British companies that had been searching the Barrett farm soon returned along the road to the bridge. After seeing the aftermath of the fighting, including the redcoat with the horrible head wound, they also hurried back to the safety of Concord, bearing the rumor that the rebels were actually scalping the British. The Americans looking down on them from the ridge held their fire.

In the hour or two it took for the British to tend to the wounded and to gather the troops into marching order, the militia numbers continued to grow. Soon the Americans outnumbered Smith's men. But Smith delayed returning to Boston, hoping his reinforcements would arrive. He knew his army was in danger of being surrounded, but he doubted the militiamen—mostly farmers untrained in the skills of battle—would start an attack in the heart of town.

At about noon, Smith decided he could wait no longer, and the British set off toward Lexington and Boston. Ready to continue the fight, some of the Americans took a shortcut over the fields to meet the British down the road. At the same time, other militia companies were also heading for the road between Concord and Lexington.

The organized march of the redcoats lasted for only the first mile. They were soon to find out just how dangerous farmers with muskets could be when aroused.

The Meriam farm lay about a mile down the road from Concord, where another road intersected it from the north. The place was called Meriam's Corner. Here the Americans, strengthened by more militia companies, which had just marched down from towns to the north, began to spread out behind stone walls and farm buildings.

They waited silently as the redcoats marched in front of them, and then began firing as the army crossed a little bridge over a brook. The redcoats in the rear returned the fire. Thus began a heated battle that continued, without stop, from Meriam's Corner to Boston.

THE BRITISH DEFENDED THEMSELVES as best they could as they moved down the road. Most had been trained to fight as a formal unit—standing up, out in the open—against an enemy fighting in the same way.

Yet here was a different kind of enemy. The militia companies were no longer organized under officers. Each man followed the British retreat from fence to wall and from tree to rock, firing, reloading, running to another bit of cover, and firing again. To some of the British, fighting from behind cover was extremely cowardly, yet the redcoats could do very little against the swarming rebels.

The British retreat quickly became an uncontrolled and desperate run to escape the guns firing at them from both sides of the road. They ran into Lexington in fearful confusion, almost out of ammunition, their bayonets useless against a hidden enemy. In Lexington they set fire to several buildings where snipers could have hidden.

Without help, not one of Colonel Smith's men ever would have reached the safety of Boston. However, even before receiving Smith's call for reinforcements, General Gage had ordered a detachment sent out to support the colonel's men. Had these troops left at the appointed time—very early in the morning—Smith's men might not have been defeated so badly, if at all. But because of several problems, the reinforcements did not get started until midmorning, which meant they encountered Smith's desperate retreat at Lexington. The fresh soldiers were a welcome sight for Smith's men.

This new detachment of about one thousand was commanded by a capable soldier: Sir Hugh Percy. On the Boston side of Lexington, Lord Percy set up defensive lines, to which Smith's exhausted men stumbled.

After less than an hour of rest for Smith's troops, Lord Percy ordered the retreat to continue. Despite the reinforcements, the danger to the British army was far from over. They had to reach the safety of Boston before dark, and fresh snipers continued to line up behind stone walls, trees, and houses as the redcoats resumed their march.

Percy had had the foresight to bring two small cannons. The cannons actually did very little harm that day, but the show of firepower did have an effect on the rebels. Whenever the British set up to fire their cannons, the Americans moved back out of range.

To help protect his men from a slaughter, Percy sent out companies of soldiers to guard the flanks, or sides, of the main army marching on the road. It was between the militiamen and these flanking soldiers that the most intense fighting took place.

In the town of Menotomy (today's Arlington), Jason Russell's house stood beside the road down which the British were retreating. Being lame, Russell was warned by friends and family to leave his home, for safety's sake. "An Englishman's home is his castle," he replied, and he stayed to help other militiamen attack the redcoats from his yard. As the retreating British approached from down the road, the Americans in Russell's yard were surprised and surrounded when flanking redcoats came up from behind the house. The only shelter for the militiamen was inside the house. The British followed them inside, killing eleven Americans. Russell was bayoneted to death outside his own front door.

When clearing other homes and barns of rebel snipers along the retreat route, the desperate redcoats sometimes killed anyone, armed or unarmed, found inside. As before, many buildings along the road were burned so snipers could not use them. Often these homes were looted before being set afire.

When a militiaman ran out of his valuable gunpowder, he had no choice but to end his part in the fighting and return home. But armed rebels continued arriving to harass the British, and the redcoats were beginning to run low on ammunition. As evening approached, the British were forced to shoot less and less, to conserve their ammunition.

With darkness only an hour away, Percy changed his mind about his route back to Boston. He turned for Charlestown, rather than Cambridge, through which his men had originally marched. He made the right choice. If he had turned toward Cambridge, his men would have come upon a large force of Americans who had taken apart the bridge there and were waiting to attack. The British would have been trapped.

Just as the last light was fading from the sky, the defeated British army stumbled into Charlestown at Boston harbor, where the powerful warships, with their rows of cannons, provided protection for the exhausted soldiers. For the British, the day of horror was finally over.

THE NEWS OF LEXINGTON AND CONCORD spread through the colonies as fast as horsemen could ride. The other colonies agreed to rise up and stand unified with the brave militiamen of Massachusetts. They sent food, arms, and soldiers to the growing army arrayed around Boston.

The British lay low in Boston, while the Americans encircled the city. Late in May, three battle-tested British generals—Sir William Howe, John Burgoyne, and Henry Clinton—arrived from England to take up command under Gage.

In June, on a hill outside of Charlestown, just across the harbor from Boston, the still largely unorganized patriots built a crude fort. Fearing the city could now be shelled, the British attacked and—with many losses—just barely defeated the patriots in the Battle of Bunker Hill. "The success is too dearly bought," commented General Howe, who would later replace Gage as commander of the British army.

The Second Continental Congress, meeting in Philadelphia that same month, commissioned George Washington to raise and train a proper American army. Despite great difficulties and a scarcity of money, General Washington proved to have

the military and, later, the political leadership the emerging country needed.

On July 4, 1776, the Congress declared America's independence from Britain. The fighting would continue for five years on land and sea, with the Americans aided by France, long an enemy of Britain. At last, in 1781, Washington's Continental Army, together with the French, trapped and laid siege to a large part of the British army and navy at Yorktown, Virginia. The British surrendered in great shame.

The American Revolution was soon over. What were once the thirteen British colonies in America became the United States of America. The difficult task of setting up a new country—one unique among all the nations of the world—would now begin.

When in the course of human events it becomes necessary for one people to dissolve the political bands which have connected them with another, and to assume among the powers of the earth the separate and equal station to which the laws of nature and of nature's god entitle them, a decent respect to the opinions of mankind requires that they should declare the causes which impel them to the separation.

We hold these truths to be self-evident; that all men are created equal; that they are endowed by their creator with certain inalienable rights; that among these are life, liberty, and the pursuit of happiness; that to secure these rights, governments are instituted among men, deriving their just powers from the consent of the governed; that whenever any form of government becomes destructive of these ends, it is the right of the people to alter or to abolish it, and to institute new government, laying its foundation on such principles and organizing its powers in such form, as to them shall seem most likely to effect their safety and happiness.

—The preamble and philosophy of government from the Declaration of Independence, *July 4, 1776.*

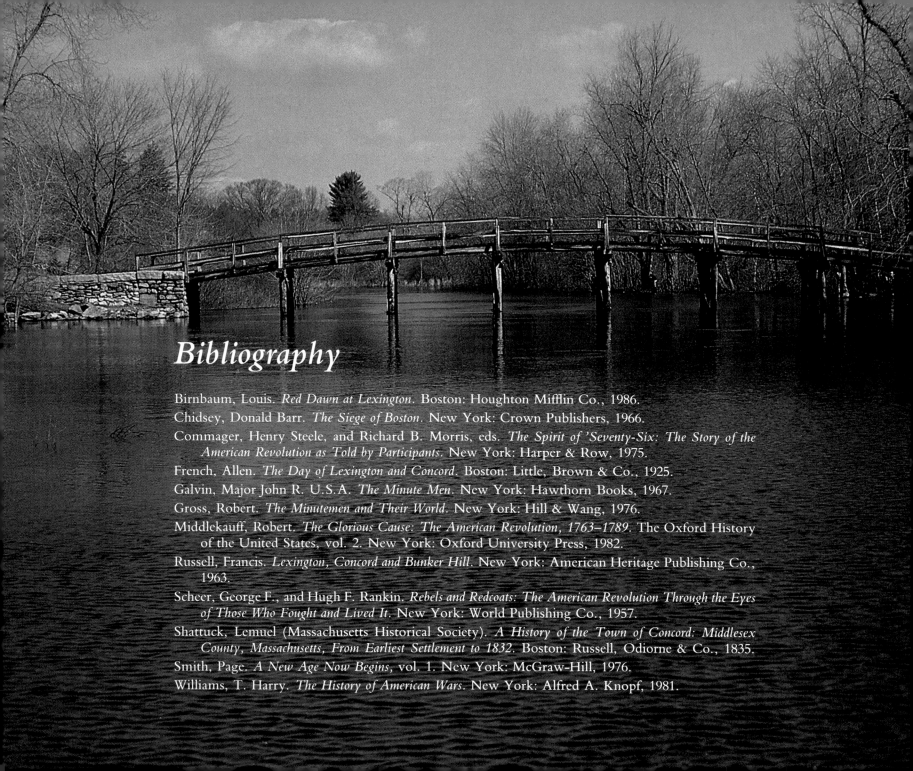

Bibliography

Birnbaum, Louis. *Red Dawn at Lexington*. Boston: Houghton Mifflin Co., 1986.

Chidsey, Donald Barr. *The Siege of Boston*. New York: Crown Publishers, 1966.

Commager, Henry Steele, and Richard B. Morris, eds. *The Spirit of 'Seventy-Six: The Story of the American Revolution as Told by Participants*. New York: Harper & Row, 1975.

French, Allen. *The Day of Lexington and Concord*. Boston: Little, Brown & Co., 1925.

Galvin, Major John R. U.S.A. *The Minute Men*. New York: Hawthorn Books, 1967.

Gross, Robert. *The Minutemen and Their World*. New York: Hill & Wang, 1976.

Middlekauff, Robert. *The Glorious Cause: The American Revolution, 1763–1789*. The Oxford History of the United States, vol. 2. New York: Oxford University Press, 1982.

Russell, Francis. *Lexington, Concord and Bunker Hill*. New York: American Heritage Publishing Co., 1963.

Scheer, George F., and Hugh F. Rankin. *Rebels and Redcoats: The American Revolution Through the Eyes of Those Who Fought and Lived It*. New York: World Publishing Co., 1957.

Shattuck, Lemuel (Massachusetts Historical Society). *A History of the Town of Concord: Middlesex County, Massachusetts, From Earliest Settlement to 1832*. Boston: Russell, Odiorne & Co., 1835.

Smith, Page. *A New Age Now Begins*, vol. 1. New York: McGraw-Hill, 1976.

Williams, T. Harry. *The History of American Wars*. New York: Alfred A. Knopf, 1981.